Here's One I Wrote Earlier
Reception and Year 1

Here's One I Wrote Earlier

Instant resources for modelled and shared writing

Reception and Year 1

Gill Matthews and Gill Howell

Learning Matters

Acknowledgements

Page 58: 'One for the Cluck of an Angry Hen', ©2000 John Foster, first published in *The Works*, compiled by Paul Cookson (Macmillan), included by permission of the author.

First published in 2002 by Learning Matters Ltd.

British Library Cataloguing in Publication Data
A CIP record for this book is available from the British Library.

ISBN 1 903300 50 9

Cover and text design by Topics – The Creative Partnership
Project management by Deer Park Productions
Typeset by Pentacor Book Design
Printed and bound in Great Britain by Ashford Colour Press

Learning Matters Ltd
58 Wonford Road
Exeter EX2 4LQ
Tel: 01392 215560
Email: info@learningmatters.co.uk
www.learningmatters.co.uk

Contents

Introduction

Here's One I Wrote Earlier, as the name suggests, offers you a substantial bank of examples of writing that you can use in modelled and shared writing sessions.

Demonstrating how to approach a particular piece of writing, or an aspect of the writing process, is an extremely effective teaching strategy. However, to think of ideas and to prepare resources for these sessions can be time consuming – and often challenging.

The examples provided here range from brief character sketches to stories to non-fiction recounts. Fiction, poetry, plays and non-fiction examples are all included. The examples are at different stages of development – from a planning frame, to an outline draft and then to a polished version – so you can use them to take children through the whole writing process.

What are modelled and shared writing?

Modelled and shared writing take place during the whole-class session of the literacy hour. They are used to demonstrate specific skills and strategies used by writers. Modelled writing involves the teacher in creating the piece of writing in front of the class. Shared writing is collaborative – the children make suggestions for content, choice of vocabulary, sentence construction, etc.

Children often think that experienced writers write perfectly all the time. It is important, therefore, that when using both teaching strategies, you talk to the children about how you write (e.g. rehearsing sentences out loud before writing them down, explaining choices of particular words and phrases, discussing possible spelling options). It is useful sometimes to make mistakes – and to demonstrate how to edit and improve a piece of writing as you write.

To keep the children interested during modelled and shared writing, you could involve them by using interactive techniques, e.g. asking questions, giving quick individual writing tasks on the whiteboard, taking time out for discussions, asking the children to come out to the front to write. Make sure that all the children can see – and reach – the writing surface. When appropriate, write on paper rather than a wipe-clean surface as this will mean the writing can be returned to for further work.

How to use this book

There are two ways to find appropriate writing examples in this book:

- Page v lists the content of the book by literacy focus. Use this page to find, for example, samples of character profiles or instructions.
- The grid on page ix lists the NLS teaching objectives covered and the relevant page references.

The writing examples are organised by term and in groups that take you through the development of a piece of writing. **All the examples in the book may be photocopied**. Some examples have been annotated so that you can use them to focus on specific teaching points (for example, pages 31, 43, 53 and 56).

Each page is organised in the same way to help you find your way around each example quickly and easily. Each example is prefaced by contextual information and is linked clearly to the NLS teaching objectives.

You'll also find suggested writing activities after each example:

 This indicates suggestions for teacher-led activities when working with the whole class.

 This indicates suggestions for activities the children could complete independently, either on their own, in pairs or in groups.

You may wish to remove the activities section at the bottom of the page and then enlarge the page, or make copies for use on an OHP. In some instances, you could give copies to the children for them to work on independently. Equally, you could use them for ideas and present them as if you had written them earlier!

Stimulus material

Wherever possible, the topics chosen for writing for each term have been linked to provide continuity. The examples are based on the identified range of texts for reading and writing in the NLS *Framework for teaching*, and some non-fiction writing has links to other curricular areas. Traditional tales and rhymes are used frequently as these provide a well-known basis that allows children to focus on the writing process rather than be diverted by unfamiliar or challenging content.

Planning grid

To aid planning, this grid refers to word, sentence and text level teaching objectives in the NLS *Framework for teaching*.

Reception

Word level	Page	Sentence level	Page	Text level	Page
		1	1, 2, 3, 4, 5, 6, 13, 14, 15, 16, 17, 18, 19	7	2, 3, 4, 5, 6, 7, 8, 9, 10, 11, 12, 14, 15, 16, 17, 18, 19, 20, 21, 22, 23, 24
		3	1, 2, 3, 4, 5, 6, 13, 14, 15, 16, 17, 18, 19	11	1, 2, 3, 4, 5, 6, 13, 14, 15, 16, 17, 18, 19, 24, 25, 26
				12	2, 3, 4, 5, 6, 14, 15, 16, 17, 18, 19, 24, 25, 26
				13	25, 26
				14	2, 3, 4, 5, 6, 7, 8, 9, 10, 11, 12, 14, 15, 16, 17, 18, 19, 20, 21, 22, 23, 24, 25, 26

Year 1 Term 1

Word level	Page	Sentence level	Page	Text level	Page
		1	1, 2, 3, 4, 5, 6, 13, 14, 15, 16, 17, 18, 19, 29, 30	3	7, 8, 9, 10, 11, 12, 20, 21, 22, 23, 24
		4	1, 2, 3, 4, 5, 6, 13, 14, 15, 16, 17, 18, 19, 29, 30	10	1, 2, 3, 4, 5, 6, 13, 14, 15, 16, 17, 18, 19
				11	1, 2, 3, 4, 5, 6, 13, 14, 15, 16, 17, 18, 19
				16	28, 29, 30, 31

Year 1 Term 2

Word level	Page	Sentence level	Page	Text level	Page
		1	32, 33, 34, 35, 36, 37, 38, 39, 42, 44	4	33, 34, 35, 36, 37, 38, 39, 40
		5	42, 44	14	32, 33, 34, 35, 36, 37, 38, 39, 40
		6	32, 33, 34, 35, 36, 37, 38	15	41
				16	32, 33, 34, 35, 36, 37, 38, 39
				25	42, 43, 44

Year 1 Term 3

Word level	Page	Sentence level	Page	Text level	Page
		1	54, 55	13	45, 46, 47, 48, 49, 50
		6	45, 46, 47, 48, 49, 50, 52, 55, 56	14	51, 52, 53
		7	57	15	58, 59, 60
				16	59, 60
				20	54, 55, 56
				22	57

**Year R
Year 1 Term 1
Fiction**

Familiar stories
Main focus Model text (see also pages 2 to 5)
NLS teaching objectives YR: S1, S3, T11/Y1: S1, S4, T10, T11

Once upon a time, there was a little girl called Little Red Riding Hood. She lived with her mother in a cottage on the edge of the wood. One day, she set off to take some cakes to her grandma.

As Little Red Riding Hood was walking through the wood, she met a wolf.
'Where are you going?' asked the wolf.
'We've baked some cakes and I'm taking them to Grandma,' said Little Red Riding Hood. She showed him the cakes and the wolf licked his lips. They did not notice the Woodcutter listening to them.

Little Red Riding Hood went into Grandma's cottage. Grandma was in bed. Little Red Riding Hood thought she looked different.
'What big ears you've got Grandma,' said Little Red Riding Hood.
'All the better to hear you with,' said the wolf.
'What big eyes you've got,' said Little Red Riding Hood.
'All the better to see you with,' said the wolf.
'What big teeth you've got,' said Little Red Riding Hood.
'All the better to eat you with,' shouted the wolf, jumping out of bed.

Just at that moment the Woodcutter rushed in. He cut open the wolf with his axe. Out jumped Grandma.
'Grandma! What happened?' cried Little Red Riding Hood.
'That horrible wolf ate me up,' said Grandma.
'Thank you for saving me, Woodcutter.'
They all had a nice cup of tea and ate the cakes that Little Red Riding Hood had brought.

Activities

- Use to re-tell the story.
- Use to demonstrate how to add sentences to pictures. Use fewer sentences if appropriate.

1

**Year R
Year 1 Term 1
Fiction**

Familiar stories
Main focus Sequencing pictures (see also pages 1 and 3 to 5)
NLS teaching objectives YR: S1, S3, T7, T11, T12, T14
Y1: S1, S4, T10, T11

Activities

- Use the pictures to demonstrate how to add sentences to pictures.

- Sequence the pictures.
- Re-tell the story orally.
- Add simple sentences to the pictures.

Year R
Year 1 Term 1
Fiction

Familiar stories
Main focus Sequencing pictures (see also pages 1, 2, 4 and 5)
NLS teaching objectives YR: S1, S3, T7, T11, T12, T14
Y1: S1, S4, T10, T11

Activity

- Use the pictures to demonstrate how to add sentences to pictures.

- Sequence the pictures.
- Re-tell the story orally.
- Add simple sentences to the pictures.

Year R
Year 1 Term 1
Fiction

Familiar stories
Main focus Sequencing pictures (see also pages 1, 2, 3 and 5)
NLS teaching objectives YR: S1, S3, T7, T11, T12, T14
Y1: S1, S4, T10, T11

Activities

- Use the pictures to demonstrate how to add sentences to pictures.

- Sequence the pictures.
- Re-tell the story orally.
- Add simple sentences to the pictures.

**Year R
Year 1 Term 1
Fiction**

Familiar stories
Main focus Sequencing pictures (see also pages 1 to 4)
NLS teaching objectives YR: S1, S3, T7, T11, T12, T14
Y1: S1, S4, T10, T11

Activities

 • Use the pictures to demonstrate how to add sentences to pictures.

 • Sequence the pictures.
• Re-tell the story orally.
• Add simple sentences to the pictures.

**Year R
Year 1 Term 1
Fiction**

Familiar stories
Main focus Writing simple sentences
NLS teaching objectives YR: S1, S3, T7, T11, T12, T14
Y1: S1, S4, T10, T11

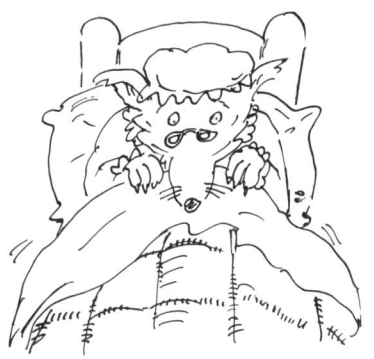

Activities

 • Use to demonstrate how to add simple sentences to pictures.

 • Use the pictures as prompts to re-tell the story.
• Write simple sentences for each picture.

Year R
Year 1 Term 1
Fiction

Familiar stories
Main focus Re-telling a familiar story (see also pages 8 to 11)
NLS teaching objective YR: T7, T14/Y1: T3

Little Red Riding Hood mask

Cut around the dotted line, then cut out the eye holes. Use a long thin piece of wood or card and attach to bottom of mask to make a handle.

Activities

 • Use to demonstrate what a character might say during the re-telling of a familiar story.

 • Use the masks to role play the story.

Year R
Year 1 Term 1
Fiction

Familiar stories
Main focus Re-telling a familiar story (see also pages 7 and 9 to 11)
NLS teaching objective YR: T7, T14/Y1: T3

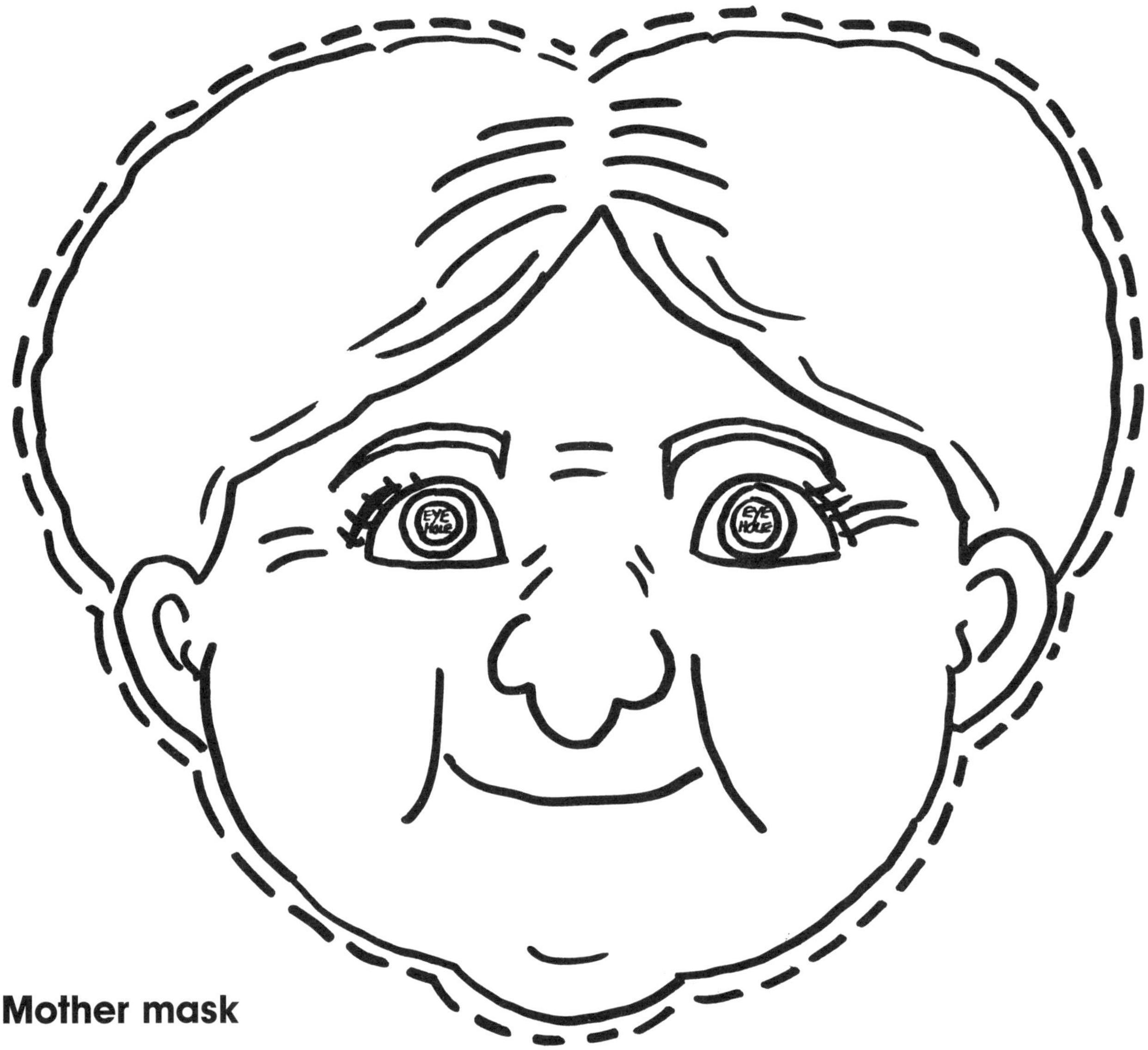

Mother mask

Cut around the dotted line, then cut out the eye holes. Use a long thin piece of wood or card and attach to bottom of mask to make a handle.

Activities

 • Use to demonstrate what a character might say during the re-telling of a familiar story.

 • Use the masks to role play the story.

**Year R
Year 1 Term 1
Fiction**

Familiar stories
Main focus Re-telling a familiar story (see also pages 7, 8, 10 and 11)
NLS teaching objective YR: T7, T14/Y1: T3

Woodcutter mask

Cut around the dotted line, then cut out the eye holes. Use a long thin piece of wood or card and attach to bottom of mask to make a handle.

EYE HOLE

EYE HOLE

Activities

• Use to demonstrate what a character might say during the re-telling of a familiar story

• Use the masks to role play the story.

**Year R
Year 1 Term 1
Fiction**

Familiar stories
Main focus Re-telling a familiar story (see also pages 7 to 9 and 11)
NLS teaching objective YR: T7, T14/Y1: T3

Grandma mask

Cut around the dotted line, then cut out the eye holes. Use a long thin piece of wood or card and attach to bottom of mask to make a handle.

Activities

 • Use to demonstrate what a character might say during the re-telling of a familiar story.

 • Use the masks to role play the story.

**Year R
Year 1 Term 1
Fiction**

Familiar stories
Main focus Re-telling a familiar story (see also pages 7 to 10)
NLS teaching objective YR: T7, T14/Y1: T3

Wolf mask

Cut around the dotted line, then cut out the eye holes. Use a long thin piece of wood or card and attach to bottom of mask to make a handle.

Activities

 • Use to demonstrate what a character might say during the re-telling of a familiar story.

 • Use the masks to role play the story.

Year R
Year 1 Term 1
Fiction

Familiar stories
Main focus Re-telling a familiar story
NLS teaching objectives YR: T7, T14/Y1: T3

Activities

- Use the story map to re-tell the story, tracing the movements of the characters.
- Write key events on Post-it notes and add them to the map.

- Draw in the characters at a particular point in the story.
- Annotate key events on the map.
- Use the story map to re-tell the story.

**Year R
Year 1 Term 1
Fiction**

Familiar stories
Main focus Model text (see also pages 14 to18)
NLS teaching objectives YR: S1, S3, T11/Y1: S1, S4, T10, T11

Once upon a time there were three bears. One day Mummy Bear made some porridge. It was too hot so the bears decided to go for a walk.

Goldilocks smelt the porridge. She was very hungry. She tried Daddy Bear's porridge but it was too hot. She tried Mummy Bear's porridge but it was too sweet. She tried Baby Bear's porridge and it was just right. She ate it all up.

Goldilocks wanted to sit down. She tried Daddy Bear's chair but it was too hard. She tried Mummy Bear's chair but it was too soft. She tried Baby Bear's chair. She was too heavy and it broke.

Goldilocks felt very tired. She tried Daddy Bear's bed but it was too hard. She tried Mummy Bear's bed but it was too soft. She tried Baby Bear's bed and it was just right. She fell fast asleep.

The bears came home. They discovered that someone had eaten Baby Bear's porridge, broken Baby Bear's chair and was fast asleep in Baby Bear's bed.
'What are you doing in Baby Bear's bed?' they all shouted. Goldilocks woke up. She was so scared that she jumped out of the window and ran home as fast as she could.

Activities

- Use to re-tell the story.
- Use as a model to demonstrate how to add sentences to pictures.
- Involve the children in adding further dialogue to the final picture.

**Year R
Year 1 Term 1
Fiction**

Familiar stories
Main focus Sequencing pictures (see also pages 13 and 15 to 18)
NLS teaching objectives YR: S1, S3, T7, T11, T12, T14
                                          Y1: S1, S4, T10, T11

Activities

- Using the pictures on pages 15 to 18, demonstrate how to sequence pictures to form a story.
- Demonstrate how to write sentences to accompany the pictures.

- Sequence this picture with those on pages 15 to 18.
- Use the pictures as the basis for re-telling the story orally.
- Add simple sentences to the pictures.

Year R
Year 1 Term 1
Fiction

Familiar stories
Main focus Sequencing pictures (see also pages 13, 14 and 16 to 18)
NLS teaching objectives YR: S1, S3, T7, T11, T12, T14
Y1: S1, S4, T10, T11

Activities

- Using the pictures on pages 14 and 16 to 18, demonstrate how to sequence pictures to form a story.
- Demonstrate how to write sentences to accompany the pictures.

- Sequence this picture with those on pages 14 and 16 to 18.
- Use the pictures as the basis for re-telling the story orally.
- Add simple sentences to the pictures.

**Year R
Year 1 Term 1
Fiction**

Familiar stories
Main focus Sequencing pictures (see also pages 13 to 15, 17 and 18)
NLS teaching objectives YR: S1, S3, T7, T11, T12, T14
Y1: S1, S4, T10, T11

Activities

- Using the pictures on pages 13 to 15, 17 and 18, demonstrate how to sequence pictures to form a story.
- Demonstrate how to write sentences to accompany the pictures.

- Sequence this picture with those on pages 13 to 15, 17 and 18.
- Use the pictures as the basis for re-telling the story orally.
- Add simple sentences to the pictures.

**Year R
Year 1 Term 1
Fiction**

Familiar stories
Main focus Sequencing pictures (see also pages 13 to 16 and 18)
NLS teaching objectives YR: S1, S3, T7, T11, T12, T14
Y1: S1, S4, T10, T11

Activities

- Using the pictures on pages 13 to 16 and 18, demonstrate how to sequence pictures to form a story.
- Demonstrate how to write sentences to accompany the pictures.

- Sequence this picture with those on pages 13 to 16 and 18.
- Use the pictures as the basis for re-telling the story orally.
- Add simple sentences to the pictures.

**Year R
Year 1 Term 1
Fiction**

Familiar stories
Main focus Sequencing pictures (see also pages 13 to 17)
NLS teaching objectives YR: S1, S3, T7, T11, T12, T14
Y1: S1, S4, T10, T11

Activities

- Using the pictures on pages 13 to 17, demonstrate how to sequence pictures to form a story.
- Demonstrate how to write sentences to accompany the pictures.

- Sequence this picture with those on pages 13 to 17.
- Use the pictures as the basis for re-telling the story orally.
- Add simple sentences to the pictures.

Year R
Year 1 Term 1
Fiction

Familiar stories
Main focus Re-telling and writing familiar stories
NLS teaching objectives YR: S1, S3, T7, T11, T12, T14
Y1: S1, S4, T10, T11

Activities

- Use to demonstrate how to add simple sentences to pictures.

- Sequence the pictures.
- Use the pictures to re-tell the story.
- Write simple sentences to accompany the pictures.

**Year R
Year 1 Term 1
Fiction**

Familiar stories
Main focus Re-telling stories
NLS teaching objective YR: T7, T14/Y1: T3

Goldilocks mask

Cut around the dotted line, then cut out the eye holes. Use a long thin piece of wood or card and attach to bottom of mask to make a handle.

Activities

 • Use the mask to demonstrate what the character might say during a re-telling of a familiar story.

 • Use the masks on pages 20 to 23 to re-tell the story.

**Year R
Year 1 Term 1
Fiction**

Familiar stories
Main focus Re-telling stories
NLS teaching objective YR: T7, T14/Y1: T3

Daddy Bear mask

Cut around the dotted line, then cut out the eye holes. Use a long thin
piece of wood or card and attach to bottom of mask to make a handle.

Activities

 • Use the mask to demonstrate what the character might say during
a re-telling of a familiar story.

 • Use the masks on pages 20 to 23 to re-tell the story.

**Year R
Year 1 Term 1
Fiction**

Familiar stories
Main focus Re-telling stories
NLS teaching objective YR: T7, T14/Y1: T3

Mummy Bear mask

Cut around the dotted line, then cut out the eye holes. Use a long thin piece of wood or card and attach to bottom of mask to make a handle.

Activities

- Use the mask to demonstrate what the character might say during a re-telling of a familiar story.

- Use the masks on pages 20 to 23 to re-tell the story.

**Year R
Year 1 Term 1
Fiction**

Familiar stories
Main focus Re-telling stories
NLS teaching objective YR: T7, T14/Y1: T3

Baby Bear mask

Cut around the dotted line, then cut out the eye holes. Use a long thin piece of wood or card and attach to bottom of mask to make a handle.

Activities

- Use the mask to demonstrate what the character might say during a re-telling of a familiar story.

- Use the masks on pages 20 to 23 to re-tell the story.

Year R
Year 1 Term 1
Fiction

Familiar story
Main focus Re-telling familiar a story
NLS teaching objectives YR: T7, T11, T12, T14/Y1: T3

Activities

- Use the story map to re-tell the story, tracing the movements of the characters.
- Write the key events of the story on Post-it notes and stick them on the story map.

- Draw in the characters at an identified point in the story.
- Annotate events on the story map.
- Use the story map to re-tell the story.

Year R Non-fiction

Recount
Main focus Writing frame (see also page 26)
NLS teaching objectives YR: T11, T12, T13, T14

Who?	Where?	When?	What?	How?

Activities

- Use the frame to discuss the five main elements of a recount: who, where, when, what, how. Enlarge as necessary to increase the width of the columns.
- Model how to add drawings, key words and/or sentences to the frame, based on your own or shared class experiences.

- Use the frame to structure own recounts.

**Year R
Non-fiction**

Recount
Main focus Model text (see also page 25)
NLS teaching objectives YR: T11, T12, T13, T14

Who?	Where?	When?	What?	How?
My family	We went to the swimming pool.	On Saturday it was a sunny day.	We had a nice swim. We had some food.	We had a lovely time.

Activity

- Use as a model to complete a structured recount.

3

2

4

1

5

By

6

Published by

ISBN

See page 61.

Year 1 Term 1
Non-fiction

Instructions
Main focus Sequencing simple instructions
NLS teaching objective T16

How to make playdough

What you need.

1 Pour the flour into a bowl.

2 Add water and oil.

3 Add the salt.

4 Add a drop of food dye.

Finally, mix it together to make dough.

Activities

 • Enlarge, cut out and demonstrate how to sequence numbered instructions.

 • Arrange the pictures in order.

Year 1 Term 1
Non-fiction

Instructions
Main focus Writing frame
NLS teaching objective S1, S4, T16

How to make playdough

What you need
What you do
1.
2.
3.
4.
Finally

Activity

- Use the frame to demonstrate how to plan and write instructions.

- Children can use the frame to structure their instructions.

Year 1 Term 1
Non-fiction

Instructions
Main focus Model text
NLS teaching objective S1, S4, T16

How to make playdough

What you need:

A mixing bowl
A wooden spoon
2 cups of flour
1 cup of water
1 cup of salt
1 tablespoon of oil
Food dye

What you do:

1. First put the flour into the bowl.
2. Add the water.
3. Add the salt and the oil.
4. Add one or two drops of food dye.

Finally, mix it all together until it forms a ball of dough.

Now you can make models with the dough and have fun!

Activities

- Use as a model for shared writing.

- Children can write instructions for making something with which they are familiar.

Year 1 Term 1
Non-fiction

Instructions
Main focus Annotated model text
NLS teaching objective T16

How to make Playdough ——————— Clear title

What you need:

A mixing bowl
A wooden spoon
2 cups of flour
1 cup of water
1 cup of salt
1 tablespoon of oil
food dye

List of what is needed at the beginning

Headings

What you do:

Time connective

1 **First** put the flour into the bowl.
2 Add the water.
3 Add the salt and the oil.
4 **Add** one or two drops of food dye.

Sequential steps

Verb at beginning of each instruction

Finally, mix it all together until it forms a ball of dough.

Clear ending of sequence with time connective

Now you can make models with the dough and have fun!

Activity

• Use to draw children's attention to the structural and linguistic features typical of instructions.

Year 1 Term 2
Fiction

Traditional stories
Main focus Model text
NLS teaching objective S1, S6, T14, T16

Once upon a time there were three little pigs. They built a house made out of straw.

A big, bad wolf came along. He huffed and puffed, and blew down the house of straw. The three little pigs ran away.

Next, the three little pigs built a house made out of sticks.

The big, bad wolf came along. He huffed and puffed and blew down the house of sticks. The three little pigs ran away.

The three little pigs built a strong house, made out of bricks. The wolf could not blow it down.

The wolf climbed down the chimney and fell into a cauldron of water. He ran away and the three little pigs lived happily ever after.

Activities

- Use to re-tell the story.
- Use to demonstrate sequencing a story.
- Use to demonstrate how to add sentences to pictures.

Year 1 Term 2
Fiction

Traditional stories
Main focus Sequencing a familiar story
NLS teaching objective S1, S6, T4, T14, T16

Activities

 • Use to demonstrate how to add sentences to illustrations.

 • Add own sentences or key words to pictures.

Year 1 Term 2
Fiction

Traditional stories
Main focus Sequencing a familiar story
NLS teaching objective S1, S6, T4, T14, T16

Activities

 • Use to demonstrate how to add sentences to illustrations.

 • Add own sentences or key words to pictures.

Year 1 Term 2
Fiction

Traditional stories
Main focus Sequencing a familiar story
NLS teaching objective S1, S6, T4, T14, T16

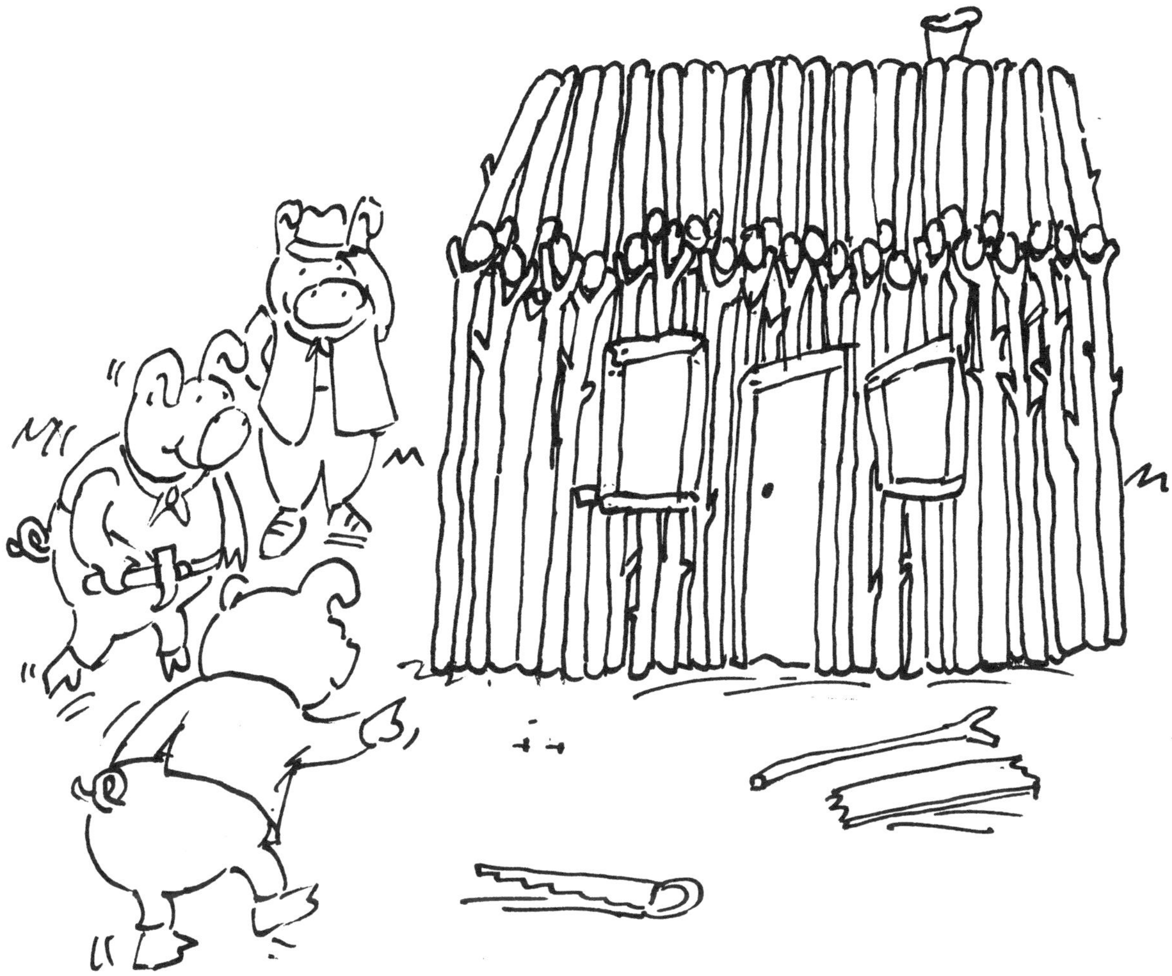

Activities

- Use to demonstrate how to add sentences to illustrations.
- Add own sentences or key words to pictures.

Year 1 Term 2
Fiction

Traditional stories
Main focus Sequencing a familiar story
NLS teaching objective S1, S6, T4, T14, T16

Activities

 • Use to demonstrate how to add sentences to illustrations.

 • Add own sentences or key words to pictures.

Year 1 Term 2
Fiction

Traditional stories
Main focus Sequencing a familiar story
NLS teaching objective S1, S6, T4, T14, T16

Activities

 • Use to demonstrate how to add sentences to illustrations.

 • Add own sentences or key words to pictures.

Traditional stories
Main focus Sequencing a familiar story
NLS teaching objective S1, S6, T4, T14, T16

Activities

 • Use to demonstrate how to add sentences to illustrations.

 • Add own sentences or key words to pictures.

Year 1 Term 2
Fiction

Traditional stories
Main focus Sequencing a familiar story
NLS teaching objective S1, T4, T14, T16

Activities

 • Demonstrate sequencing story and re-telling in own words.

 • Re-tell the story in sequence, using own words.

Year 1 Term 2
Fiction

Traditional stories Fairy stories; stories with familiar, predictable and patterned language
Main focus Story map
NLS teaching objectives T4, T14

Activities

- Re-tell the story following the story map.
- Write key events of the story on Post-it notes and stick them on the story map.

- Re-tell the story in own words following the story map.

Year 1 Term 2
Fiction

Traditional stories
Main focus Character profile
NLS teaching objectives T15

Who am I?

I am grey and very hairy.
I have big, sharp teeth.
I have big, pointed ears and a long, furry tail.
I have sharp claws.
I eat fat little pigs, little girls in red capes, and little goats and kids.
I live in the forest.

I am a big, bad wolf!

Year 1 Term 2
Non-fiction

Simple reports
Main focus Model text
NLS teaching objective S1, S5, T25

Fairy Tale Wolves

Ever since fairy stories were first told, there have been big, bad wolves in the stories.

These wolves are big and grey, and very hungry. They try to eat weak, young fairy-tale characters. They often trick the characters by pretending to be someone else. If they have fooled the characters, they will eat them.

Big, bad wolves appear in these fairy stories:

• Little Red Riding Hood
• The Three Little Pigs
• The Wolf and the Seven Little Kids

In *Little Red Riding Hood*, the woodcutter came to the grandmother's cottage and killed the wolf.
The wolf in *The Three Little Pigs* fell down the chimney into a cauldron of hot water and ran away.
In *The Wolf and the Seven Little Kids*, Mother Goat rescued the kids.

In fairy stories, the wolf never wins, and they all live happily ever after.

Activities

 • Use as a model of a simple report.

 • Children can write simple reports about familiar animal characters.

Year 1 Term 2
Non-fiction

Simple reports
Main focus Annotated model text – report
NLS teaching objective T25

Fairy Tale Wolves —————— Title

Ever since fairy stories were first told, there have been
(big, bad wolves) in the stories.

Generalised
participants

General opening statement

These wolves are big and grey, and very hungry. They try to
eat weak, young fairy-tale characters. They often trick the
characters by pretending to be someone else. (If they have
fooled the characters, they will eat them.)

Non-specific
information
about fairy-tale
wolves in general

Big, bad wolves appear in these fairy stories:

- Little Red Riding Hood
- The Three Little Pigs
- The Wolf and the Seven Little Kids

Bullet
point
list

In *Little Red Riding Hood*, the woodcutter came to the
grandmother's cottage and killed the wolf.
The wolf in *The Three Little Pigs* fell down the chimney
into a cauldron of hot water and ran away.
In *The Wolf and the Seven Little Kids*, Mother Goat
(rescued the kids)

Specific
detail

In fairy stories, the wolf never wins, and (they all live happily
ever after.)

Generalised closing
statement

Activity

- Use annotations to illustrate points to aid writing own reports.

Year 1 Term 2
Non-fiction

Simple reports
Main focus Writing frame
NLS teaching objective S1, S5, T25

Title of report
Opening
Details • • •
Closing

 • Use in modelled and shared writing to demonstrate report writing.

 • Use to support beginning of report writing/drafts.

Year 1 Term 3
Fiction

Familiar stories
Main focus Model text (see also pages 46 and 47)
NLS teaching objectives S6, T13

One day Jack took the cow to market. He wanted to sell her.

On his way, he met an old man. Jack swapped the cow for five beans.

Jack's mother told him he was very stupid. She threw the beans out of the window.

The next day, there was a huge beanstalk right outside the window.

Activities

- Use these illustrations and those on pages 46 and 47 to demonstrate how to record significant events in a known story using story language. Focus particularly on the use of sentences.

- Use pages 45 to 47, with or without the text, to sequence and re-tell the story.
- Record significant events in a different story.

Year 1 Term 3
Fiction

Familiar stories
Main focus Model text (see also pages 45 and 47)
NLS teaching objectives S6, T13

Jack climbed up the beanstalk. He climbed up and up, right to the top. At the top of the beanstalk was a huge castle.

Jack crept into the castle. He saw a giant counting gold coins.

When the giant fell asleep, Jack picked up one of the sacks of money. He climbed down the beanstalk and showed the money to his mother.

Jack climbed the beanstalk again. He crept into the castle. This time he saw a hen laying a golden egg.

Activities

- Use these illustrations and those on pages 45 and 47 to demonstrate how to record significant events in a known story using story language. Focus particularly on the use of sentences.

- Use pages 45 to 47, with or without the text, to sequence and re-tell the story.
- Record significant events in a different story.

Year 1 Term 3

Fiction

Familiar stories
Main focus Model text (see also pages 45 and 46)
NLS teaching objectives S6, T13

When the giant fell asleep, Jack picked up the hen. He climbed down the beanstalk and showed the hen to his mother.

Jack climbed the beanstalk again. He crept into the castle. This time he saw a singing golden harp.

When the giant fell asleep, Jack picked up the harp. It cried out and woke the giant. The giant chased Jack down the beanstalk.

When Jack reached the bottom of the beanstalk, he chopped it down. The giant hit the ground and was killed. Jack and his mother lived happily ever after with their money, their hen and their harp.

Activities

- Use these illustrations and those on pages 45 and 46 to demonstrate how to record significant events in a known story using story language. Focus particularly on the use of sentences.

- Use pages 45 to 47, with or without the text, to sequence and re-tell the story.
- Record significant events in a different story.

Year 1 Term 3
Fiction

Familiar stories
Main focus Structuring and recording main events (see also pages 49 and 50)
NLS teaching objectives S6, T13

Activities

 • Use these illustrations, and those on pages 49 and 50, to demonstrate how to structure and re-tell the main events in a known story. Involve the children in writing the key events that accompany each illustration.

 • Structure and record the main events in a known story, and use the illustrations as prompts to re-tell the story.

Year 1 Term 3
Fiction

Familiar stories
Main focus Structuring and recording main events (see also pages 48 and 50)
NLS teaching objectives S6, T13

Activities

 • Use these illustrations, and those on pages 48 and 50, to demonstrate how to structure and re-tell the main events in a known story. Involve the children in writing the key events that accompany each illustration.

 • Structure and record the main events in a known story.
• Use the illustrations as prompts to re-tell the story.

Year 1 Term 3
Fiction

Familiar stories
Main focus Structuring and recording main events (see also pages 48 and 49)
NLS teaching objectives S6, T13

Activities

- Use these illustrations, and those on pages 48 and 49, to demonstrate how to structure and re-tell the main events in a known story. Involve the children in writing the key events that accompany each illustration.

- Use these illustrations, and those on pages 48 and 49, to structure and record the main events in a known story.
- Use the illustrations as prompts to re-tell the story.

Year 1 Term 3
Fiction

Simple settings
Main focus Describing settings (see also pages 52 and 53)
NLS teaching objective T14

Activity

- Use the illustration as the stimulus for writing a description of a setting in preparation for writing a story.

Year 1 Term 3
Fiction

Simple settings
Main focus Model text (see also page 53)
NLS teaching objective S6, T14

The castle was enormous. At one end of the cold, dark room there was a huge table with two large chairs. There was a threadbare rug on the floor. A tiny flame flickered in the fireplace. The sound of footsteps suddenly echoed around the room. The floor began to shake.

Activities

 • Use the model text to demonstrate how to write a description of a setting. Focus on using the senses. Encourage the children to identify what can be seen, heard and felt.

 • Children can write their own setting descriptions.

Year 1 Term 3
Fiction

Simple settings
Main focus Annotated model text (see also page 52)
NLS teaching objective T14

Where

Adjectives used to add detail

What can be seen

What can be felt

What can be heard

The castle was enormous. At one end of the cold, dark room there was a huge table with two large chairs. There was a threadbare rug on the floor. A tiny flame flickered in the fireplace. The sound of footsteps suddenly echoed around the room. The floor began to shake.

Activities

- Use to explore features of setting descriptions, e.g. where it is, use of the senses, adjectives, etc.

Year 1 Term 3
Non-fiction

Recount Writing frame
Main focus Planning a recount
NLS teaching objective S1, T20

Who?	Where?	When?	What?	How?

Activities

 • Use the writing frame to demonstrate how to structure recounts and what kind of information to include. Enlarge as necessary to increase the width of the columns.

 • Use the frame to structure and plan own recounts.

Year 1 Term 3
Non-fiction

Recount
Main focus Model text
NLS teaching objectives S1, S6, T20

Four months ago, our class planted beans. We each planted one bean in a plant pot filled with soil. We watered our plant pots every day. After about two weeks, I could see a little green shoot pushing through the soil in my plant pot. The next week, a leaf grew on the shoot. It was very pale green. After two months my bean plant had 10 leaves and was nearly 20cm tall. One month later, I planted my bean plant in the garden. There were lots of flowers on it. Then the flowers died and in their place were little pods. Yesterday I picked lots of the pods. Inside the pods were some green beans. Last night we ate the beans with our tea. I thought they were delicious.

Activities

- Use the model text to demonstrate how to structure and write a recount. Draw children's attention to the use of time words and phrases. Focus particularly on writing in sentences.

- If the recount is copied and cut into separate sentences, children can reconstruct the text.

Year 1 Term 3
Non-fiction

Recount
Main focus Annotated model text
NLS teaching objectives S6, T20

Time connectives

When

Who

Four months ago, my class planted beans. We each planted one bean in a plant pot filled with soil. We watered our plant pots every day. After about two weeks, I could see a little green shoot pushing through the soil in my plant pot. The next week, a leaf grew on the shoot. It was very pale green. After two months my bean plant had 10 leaves and was nearly 20cm tall. One month later I planted my bean plant in the garden. There were lots of flowers on it. Then the flowers died and in their place were little pods. Yesterday I picked lots of the pods. Inside the pods were some green beans. Last night we ate the beans with our tea. I thought they were delicious.

How the writer responded

What happened in chronological order

Past tense

Past tense

Activity

 • Use the model text to demonstrate how to structure and write a recount. Draw children's attention to the use of time words and phrases. Focus particularly on writing in sentences.

56

Year 1 Term 3
Non-fiction

Research skills
Main focus Recording information
NLS teaching objectives S7, T22

What I know	What I would like to know	What I have learned

Activities

- Use the grid to demonstrate how to record existing knowledge about a topic, pose questions and record the answers after research. Enlarge as necessary to increase the width of the columns. Focus particularly in adding question marks to questions.

- Use the grid during research.

Year 1 Term 3
Fiction

Poetry
Main focus Stimulus poem
NLS teaching objective T15

One for the Cluck of an Angry Hen

One for the cluck of an angry hen.
Two for the cheeps of a tiny wren.
Three for the croak of a fat green frog.
Four for the bark of a jumping dog.
Five for the quack of a duck on a lake.
Six for the hiss of a wriggling snake.
Seven for the hoot of the old grey owl.
Eight for the snarl of a wolf on the prowl.
Nine for the squeak of a scuttling rat.
Ten for the purr of a snuggling cat.

John Foster

Activity

- With the children, explore and identify the rhyme pattern and structure of this poem.

Year 1 Term 3
Fiction

Poetry
Main focus Writing frame
NLS teaching objective T15, T16

One for the ....

One for the ....

Two for the ....

Three for the ....

Four for the ....

Five for the ....

Six for the ....

Seven for the ....

Eight for the ....

Nine for the ....

Ten for the ....

Activities

 • Use the frame to plan and demonstrate how to write a poem based on the stimulus poem (page 58). Focus particularly on the rhyming pattern and structure (see model text on page 60).

 • Use the frame to plan and write their own poems.

Year 1 Term 3
Fiction

Poetry
Main focus Model text
NLS teaching objectives T15, T16

One for the Buzz of a Stripy Bee

One for the buzz of a stripy bee.
Two for the jump of a tiny flea.
Three for the trail of a slow, slow snail.
Four for the song of a lonely whale.
Five for the whistle of a yellow parrot.
Six for the sight of a rabbit with a carrot.
Seven for the bounce of a kangaroo.
Eight for the animals in a zoo.
Nine for the honk of an old grey goose.
Ten for the bellow of an angry moose.

Activity

- Use to demonstrate how to write a poem based on the stimulus poem (page 58). Focus particularly on the rhyming pattern and structure.

Origami book

1 Photocopy page 27 and enlarge to A3.

2 Fold photocopied sheet in half lengthways, keeping the text on the outside.

3 Open out the sheet and fold in half widthways keeping the text on the outside.

4 Cut along the dotted line. Open out.

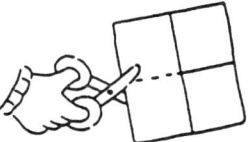

5 Fold along the remaining solid lines. This time the text is on the inside. Open out.

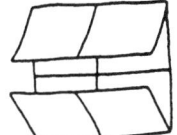

6 Fold lengthways once more, keeping the text on the outside.

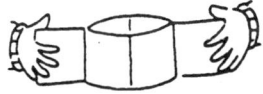

7 Hold in this position and in one movement fold as shown.

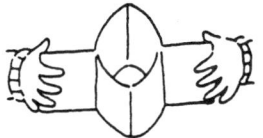

8 Fold into a book shape, with title at the front.